I READ! YOU READ!

Child's Turn to Read

Adult's Turn to Read

WE READ ABOUT

DOGS

Douglas Bender and Madison Parker

TABLE OF CONTENTS

Words to Know 3

Sight Words 3

Index 16

SEAHORSE PUBLISHING

Parent and Caregiver Guide

Reading aloud with your child has many benefits. It expands vocabulary, sparks discussion, and promotes an emotional bond. Research shows that children who have books read aloud to them have improved language skills, leading to greater school success.

I Read! You Read! books offer a fun and easy way to read with your child. Follow these guidelines.

Before Reading

- Look at the front and back covers. Discuss personal experiences that relate to the topic.
- Read the *Words to Know* on page 3. Talk about what the words mean.
- If the book will be challenging or unfamiliar to your child, read it aloud by yourself the first time. Then, invite your child to participate in a second reading.

During Reading

CHILD Have your child read the words beside this symbol. This text has been carefully matched to the reading and grade levels shown on the cover.

ADULT You read the words beside this symbol.

- Stop often to discuss what you are reading and to make sure your child understands.
- If your child struggles with decoding a word, help them sound it out. If it is still a challenge, say the word for your child and have them repeat it after you.
- To find the meaning of a word, look for clues in the surrounding words and pictures.

After Reading

- Praise your child's efforts. Notice how they have grown as a reader.
- Ask and answer questions about the book.
- Discuss what your child learned and what they liked or didn't like about the book.

Most importantly, let your child know that reading is fun and worthwhile. Keep reading together as your child's skills and confidence grow.

WORDS TO KNOW

dog

dog food

tails

treats

tricks

SIGHT WORDS

a	big	have	some
all	can	is	this
and	do	like	
are	eat	little	

This is a **dog**.

CHILD

Dogs are mammals. Mammals have fur and make milk for their babies.

ADULT

dog

Some dogs are big, and some are little.

CHILD

Dogs can be small, medium, or large.

ADULT

CHILD

All dogs eat **dog food**.

ADULT

Dog food gives dogs nutrients and energy to be active and healthy.

Some dogs can do **tricks**!

CHILD

It takes a lot of training and practice to teach a dog to do **tricks**.

ADULT

trick

Some dogs have **tails**. CHILD

When dogs wag their **tails**, it means they are happy or excited about something. ADULT

tails

All dogs like **treats.**

CHILD

Giving **treats** can reward dogs for good behavior.

ADULT

treats

INDEX

big 6
dog(s) 4, 5, 6, 8, 10, 12, 14
eat 8
little 6
tails 12, 13
treats 14, 15
trick(s) 10, 11

Written by: Douglas Bender and Madison Parker
Design by: Under the Oaks Media
Series Development: James Earley
Editor: Kim Thompson

Photos:
Shutterstock: ESB Professional: cover; xkundova: p. 5; Alberto Hernandez Leva: p. 7; Alex_ugalek: p. 9; dezy: p. 11; ayorch: p. 13; Javier Brosch

Library of Congress PCN Data
We Read About Dogs / Douglas Bender and Madison Parker
I Read! You Read!
ISBN 979-8-8873-5187-2(hard cover)
ISBN 979-8-8873-5207-7(paperback)
ISBN 979-8-8873-5227-5(EPUB)
ISBN 979-8-8873-5247-3(eBook)
Library of Congress Control Number: 2022945527

Printed in China

Seahorse Publishing Company
www.seahorsepub.com

Published in the United States
Seahorse Publishing
PO Box 771325
Coral Springs, FL 33077

SEAHORSE PUBLISHING